Trying on Bathing Suits & Other Horror Stories

Trying on Bathing Suits & Other Horror Stories

by

Lois Podoshen

© Copyright 2012 by Lois Podoshen

All rights reserved. No part of this book may be reproduced, stored in a retrieval system or transmitted in any form or by any means without prior written permission of the author, except by a reviewer who may quote brief passages in reviews to be printed in a newspaper, magazine, journal, or on-line bookseller.

ISBN-13: 978-1481132114 / ISBN-10: 1481132113

Cover Photograph by Dreamstime.com®
Cover Design by Mary Lois Sanders

Dedicated

To all people who love to laugh,
especially at themselves!

Disclaimer

This book is creative nonfiction. Some names and places have been changed to protect the humorous. Any resemblance to serious persons, living or dead, is purely coincidental!

CONTENTS

To Pee or Not to Pee 1
The Eyes Have It 5
Suburban Safari 9
Real Women Don't Sweat 15
Nuts to You 19
Childish 25
Potted 29
Leaf Me Alone 35
No Sale 39
Basic Training 45
Trying on Bathing Suits 51
Final Resting Place 57
Do, Re, Mi and DNA 63
Chicken Soup in August 71
Roll Over, Beethoven 77
John Wayne to the Rescue 85
Arugula 89
It's Just a Number 95
Paul Newman Made Me Do It 99
ET, Phone Home Plate 105
Spam I Am 113
A Full Nest 117
Discussion Guide 122

Trying on Bathing Suits   1

To Pee or Not to Pee

Okay, I admit it. I'm a woman with penis envy! No, not all the time, just certain times, like when I'm twenty-fifth in line for the ladies' room during the intermission of the Broadway production of *Jersey Boys*. It upsets me to hop from foot to foot for what seems like hours while watching my husband zip right in and out of the men's room in a millisecond.

While women on the bathroom line grumble, their husbands, boyfriends and lovers mill around the hallways with a smug sense of superiority tempered only by the Kate Spade purses that they hold for their female companions. Some men use this time to consult their iPhones, check their email, get their messages or read the *Playbill* from cover to cover. But whatever they're doing, they all have the same expression on their faces that says, "What do these women do in there that takes so long?"

Like most women, I am convinced that all architects are men and have no clue how to design an efficient and adequate ladies' room. They simply don't understand how time consuming it is to manipulate buttons and hooks and spandex.

While vacationing in France a couple of years ago, my husband and I visited the Musée D'Orsay, and after a full morning of viewing Renoirs and Monets, we needed to use the water closet. As my husband sauntered into the men's room, I became number thirty-three on the ladies' room line that snaked its way down a flight of stairs. I watched as each succeeding woman joined the line and in her native tongue yelled, "Mon Dieu!" "Dios Mio!" or "Good God!" Whether they wore silky saris, filmy French dresses or tank tops and jeans, when they finally reached the Promised Land and realized that there were only two stalls, their faces all wore the universal expression: "What man designed this bathroom?"

My toilette experiences in France would only get worse. After taking pictures in a charming little town called Tarascon, it was that time again. Luckily, we found a public toilet that had no line. I was ecstatic, but my joy was short-lived when I realized that not only didn't the bathroom have a line, it had no toilet, just a hole in the ground.

"Michael," I screamed to my husband on the other side, "there's no toilet in here."

"I know," he said, "you have to squat."

"What?" I responded incredulously. I looked down at the hole and realized that I really didn't know how to squat. My mother taught me that little boys stand up and little girls sit down and there was never, ever any discussion about squatting. Besides, this was France, one of the most civilized countries in the world, not some third-world nation. This was France, a country known for its bidets, for God sakes! And here I was trying to figure out how to pee in a hole in the ground.

"Do I squat facing the hole or with my backside to it?" I asked Michael, as if he were the expert.

"Whatever works for you," he said.

The trouble was, nothing worked for me. I left with my bladder empty but my pants' legs wet. As we drove back to our hotel, how I envied my husband with his dry pants and his dignity intact.

I really don't want to change my anatomy, but when I'm standing in the bathroom line I wonder what it would be like to take just two minutes to do my business. And to all the men out there who wonder what we do in there that takes so long, I say, "Walk a mile in my pantyhose! Drink a cup of coffee, put on a pair of control tops and a body suit and stand in line for the ladies' room during intermission of *Wicked*. You'll find out."

The Eyes Have It

Like the cleft in his chin and his crooked front tooth, they had been part of who he was for most of his life. They were the first things he reached for in the morning and the last things he took off at night. They enabled him to revel at our children's faces just moments after they were born and to *ooh* and *ah* at a romantic sunset on Waikiki Beach.

And it was with a flourish and an exclamation of "Free at last!" that my husband threw his glasses away, never to be worn again. But his road to optical freedom was not without obstacles.

"Your lens refraction and the size of your pupils show that you are a good candidate for the latest Lasik procedure to correct your nearsightedness," said the ophthalmologist when he examined Michael.

Unfortunately, I wasn't a good candidate's wife. As the doctor explained how the laser would cut a flap in Michael's cornea, I could feel my stomach churn as the acid roiled up my esophagus. The thought of anything cutting into his beautiful baby blues was just too repulsive and scary for me. Even though Michael had done his homework, read all the literature, surfed the Net, knew the difference between the flying spot and the up and down laser and had chosen a doctor whose success rate was admirable, I still had reservations.

"What if something goes wrong?" I asked him. "This seems a pretty radical solution to a problem that is easily corrected by glasses."

"You don't understand," he said.

And he was right! I didn't understand since I had perfect vision and needed no assistance to see a hawk flying high in the distance or read the ingredients on my cereal box in the morning.

"With this surgery," he said, "there will be no more glasses to fog up when I'm skiing and no more painful red dents chiseled into the sides of my nose by ill-fitting eyewear, and no more asking you to find room in your purse for my three pairs of glasses."

Now he had my attention. How many times had I gotten dents in my shoulder from carrying around all his eyeglasses in my overstuffed Louis Vuitton? How many times had I begged him to buy a fanny pack to accommodate his ever-expanding collection of eyewear—consisting of glasses for distance, glasses for close-up, old prescription, new prescription and tinted glasses for the sun? He won me over.

Several weeks later we found ourselves at the office of Dr. Seewell and his amazing laser, waiting for him to perform his magic. Similarly afflicted people eagerly awaited the miracle of unassisted sight. The place had a mystical quality—something akin to Lourdes. Any moment I expected a patient to come out of the operating room, throw away a pair of glasses, raise his arms upward and sing *Ave Maria*.

The nurse came into the waiting room, called Michael's name and then turned to me.

"You're welcome to watch the procedure," she cheerily said.

"I think I'll pass," I said as my heart pounded and my palms started to sweat.

"Mr. Podoshen," she said, "would you like a tranquilizer before we start?"

Michael quickly declined, but in a small trembling voice I said, "I'll take it!"

To my relief, less than an hour later Michael reappeared smiling, wearing protective wrap-around glasses and carrying prophylactic eye drops that would prevent infection and dryness. He proudly announced to everyone within earshot that his sight was now 20/30 and was expected to be even better by week's end. As we walked to the door, he happily stopped to throw his now unnecessary glasses into the bin provided. I quickly rummaged through my purse to find his other three pairs. Flinging them into the receptacle, I bowed my head and whispered, "Thank you God"—for my husband's sight—and for the new little suede clutch I'm going to buy at Bloomies.

Suburban Safari

Any mother of teenage boys will tell you that coming home and being greeted by your sons at the front door is never a good sign.

"Oh my God, what's wrong?" I screamed as I threw open the car door and ran from the driveway to the house.

"Mom," Jeff said barring my way, "you really don't want to go in there!"

In my mind, I conjured up the worst catastrophes I could think of. Did the toilet backup spewing sewage all over my new carpet? Did the washing machine overflow?

"A fire, was there a fire?" I asked, as I barreled past them into the house to look around and assess the damage.

"Mom," my younger son Lawrence said, "we don't know how to tell you this, but there's a snake in the house!"

I paled. My knees buckled. My heart nearly stopped. If there is one thing you don't tell your born-and-bred-in-the-wilds-of-Brooklyn mother, who even refuses to go into the reptile house at the Bronx Zoo, it's that there is a snake in her house.

It had taken years for this transplanted city girl to get used to cohabitating with birds that thoughtlessly awakened me at the crack of dawn every morning, and the rabbits that feasted on my impatiens for breakfast. And I had never gotten used to the idea that snakes dared to exist on the grounds of my suburban home. Now I was faced with the possibility that one of them actually had the audacity to enter it.

Trying to regain my composure, I shouted, "Get me my Mylanta and make it a double. And if this is some kind of ploy you guys cooked up to get us to buy you a kitten, let me tell you right now, this is not going to work."

"Don't worry, Mom, he's just a garter snake and won't hurt you," Lawrence said. "We've got him cornered behind the bookcase."

I glowered at the bookcase wondering which of the heavy tomes had lured the snake to our abode. Was it *Zen in the Art of Archery*? *Golf Tips of the Pros*? or *The Second Jewish Book of Why*? Chug-a-lugging Mylanta all the way, I quickly retreated up the two flights of stairs to the kitchen and safety. And there I stood for over an hour pacing and fretting until my husband, my fearless warrior, returned home to rescue his damsel in distress.

When he finally came through the door, I screamed, "Thank God you're home. There's a snake in the house."

"What kind?" he asked.

"What kind? The kind that's supposed to be in the yard and not in the house scaring me!"

"It's just a garter snake, Dad," said Lawrence.

"We'll look for it after dinner. Let's eat," my husband replied.

"No one is eating until that snake is found," I said as I retreated into the safety of our bedroom.

With that, my three hungry warriors donned their Rossignol® ski boots and, armed with a nine iron, a putter and a Big Bertha, stealthily sought out the interloper whom I had named "Sammy". The now infamous bookcase was moved only to reveal that our slippery friend had out-snaked us.

"I'm not staying in this house until that snake is found," I said, looking through the yellow pages to find the phone number of the nearest motel and wondering if Mylanta came in 2-liter bottles.

Knowing I meant every word, my warriors

called an animal control specialist who told us the only way to catch Sammy was to put down glue traps. He assured me that the chances of Sammy climbing the two flights of stairs to the bedrooms were extremely remote. I didn't know if this was the truth or if my husband had paid him to say it so I wouldn't take a room at the Hilton.

"He'll come out when he's hungry," the specialist said.

"How long do you think that might be?" I asked.

"Could be two weeks, call me when he reappears," he said as he laid the sticky glue traps in our family room.

I gave up the idea of a two-week hotel stay but yelled, "I am not going down there until that snake is caught." But as I looked at the glue traps in front of my washer and dryer, I knew I had a problem. I left the house and headed straight to Victoria's Secret to purchase two week's worth of underwear. This was war! And I was going to show Sammy that I was in for the long haul.

Returning home loaded down with my supplies, which consisted of fourteen pairs of Victoria's finest panties, none of which were in animal prints, a terrible thought hit me. How was I going to tell my brother and his family, who were coming from Maryland to spend the weekend, that the guest rooms were in occupied territory? I dialed their number and tried to adopt an upbeat, nonchalant air.

"Hi Cathy," I said to my sister-in-law, "Guess who's coming to dinner?"

"Sidney Poitier?" she asked.

"No, Sammy the Snake," I chirped.

"Sammy the Snake? You invited a member of the Sopranos to have dinner with us?" she asked.

I told her the snake story and hoped that my brother was standing next to her when she fell.

"Don't worry, we'll just double up in the upstairs bedrooms with my kids where the snake can't get us," I assured her, not really believing this myself. And the next evening they arrived — my brother, his wife, their crying infant and their overtired four-year-old. Lawrence took one look at this road-weary group, wrapped himself in a blanket, scooped up his pillow and announced loudly, "I'll take my chances with the snake," as he headed downstairs.

The snake, thankfully, did not appear that weekend, nor did it appear anytime during that two-week period of playing hide and seek. My husband continued to go downstairs to use the computer and my sons went downstairs to listen to music without encountering my nemesis.

But by the end of two weeks, I was desperate—I was running out of clean underwear. Hoping that Sammy was on a diet or had enough reading material to keep him busy for a while, I cautiously ventured down the stairs. As I put my foot on the first step, I saw something sticking out of one of the glue traps. Before I fainted, Sammy and I both looked at each other and yelled, "Gotcha!"

Real Women Don't Sweat

I hate exercise. No, hate is much too mild a word. I loathe exercise! So imagine the horror I felt when my doctor whipped out her prescription pad and penned the following notation: strenuous, weight-bearing exercise for 30 minutes, three times a week.

"This," she said, "is the requisite prophylaxis for osteoporosis, stroke, heart attack and all the other maladies that can befall a woman your age."

For someone like me—whose relaxation mantra is "Real women don't sweat", who wouldn't consider wearing a thong and doesn't own a pair of cross-trainers—filling this prescription was going to be a challenge.

My well-meaning, marathon-running husband suggested I buy an exercise video so I could moan and groan in the privacy of our home and not embarrass myself.

"But," I said, "How will Jane Fonda know if I'm tightening my glutes properly while exhaling? Will Cindy Crawford be able to tell how many sets of bicep curls are right for me? And more importantly, will Suzanne Summers know that I have put down my "soup can weights" and that I'm now ironing while watching *her* do pelvic tilts?"

On the advice of a friend, I decided to call a personal trainer. I phoned the local club and made an appointment with Tawny. Why is it, I thought to myself, that personal trainers are always named Tawny or Blake instead of Tom, Dick or Mary? Do their mothers know the moment they're born that they'll always look good in spandex and have a propensity for doing repetitive tasks without getting carpal tunnel or tennis elbow?

After making an appointment with Tawny, I decided to tackle the real challenge —what I was going to wear.

I quickly rummaged through my drawers to find my soft fleece sweat pants. These well-worn, treasured pants are usually reserved for when I have the flu or after a bad day at the office when all I want to do is climb into bed with Mallomars® or Ben and Jerry's Cherry Garcia® ice cream. But upon careful examination, I decided these sweat pants were definitely not "club" worthy. I threw open my closet and prayed I would find something, anything that even remotely resembled spandex. Finding nothing, I settled on a pair of loose fitting shorts and my son's Georgia Tech t-shirt, which I coupled with a pair of sneakers left over from my last foray into physical fitness—"Sweating to the Oldies" with Richard Simmons.

The moment-of-truth arrived that Friday when I cautiously walked into the gym to meet Tawny who was thoughtfully dressed in a loose fitting tracksuit that covered what I knew was a very buff body. To my horror, she informed me that we would start out with a fitness assessment test.

God, I begged, let me take the math section of the GREs, or the New York State medical exam. Ask me to explain the big bang theory, but please, please do not give me a fitness assessment test! I thought of using an old ploy that had always worked on my high school gym teacher but somehow, I didn't think Tawny was going to buy the "wrong time of the month" excuse.

Undaunted by my protestations, she hooked me up to a computer that spewed out precious data about my heart beat, pulse, respiration and strength while I huffed and puffed on the treadmill and stationary bicycle. I couldn't see the numbers, but I could tell by the pained look on Tawny's face that I would be lucky if my doctor didn't double my prescription.

"We're going to start," Tawny announced, "with circuit training." In no time at all, she had me doing leg extensions for my quadriceps, standing leg curls for my hamstrings and abductor leg raises for my *gluteus medius* and tensor thigh muscles. I was pumped. After awhile, the cold metal of the weights touching my bare skin began to empower me. I started speaking with an Austrian accent.

It was while I was fantasizing about starring in "Terminator V" that I felt it—a warm, moist, clammy feeling spreading down my back and under my arms.

"Oh my God," I said to Tawny, "can this really be happening?" There on my arm, as testimony to my hard work, were round, glistening, globules of honest-to-goodness, glorious sweat!

"Move over Schwarzenegger," I loudly exclaimed, "here I come!"

Nuts to You

"Guess what I had for lunch today?" my husband asked, arriving home from work.

"Something good, I hope," I answered.

"Chopped goat lungs."

"Chopped goat lungs? Um, sounds yummy!"

"Tony took me out for Philippine food. It was really different. Oh, by the way, I brought you a present from the Philippine Bread House."

"It better not be goat's lungs," I said, as I watched him remove a plastic container from his attaché case.

"It's nuts—glazed *pili* nuts, a Philippine delicacy."

"Thanks," I said. I gave him a hug while thinking to myself, "Is *he* nuts?" I have great willpower, but there are two things in this world I simply can't resist—Entenmann's® chocolate covered doughnuts and nuts, any kind of nuts— Brazil nuts, peanuts, filberts, macadamias, almonds, cashews. I love nuts in any form—dry roasted, salted, in the shell, out of the shell, nuts in ice cream, nuts in fudge, nuts in granola, straight from the can, or in this case, straight out of the plastic container from The Philippine Bread House. Nuts, glorious nuts; fat laden, mega-calorie nuts are my downfall.

What was he thinking? Just last month I asked him for a treadmill for my birthday. A treadmill! When was the last time I ever asked for anything metal that didn't have 14K embossed on it? When had I ever asked for anything having to do with sweat that didn't come with plane tickets and piña coladas? When had I ever asked for anything with a motor that didn't have heated seats and a moon roof? Was he trying to sabotage my fitness program?

I picked up the container and looked at the glazed morsels. Thinking that they weren't as deadly as they looked, I read the ingredients— *pili* nuts, coconut oil and sugar syrup. Each serving contained 350 calories and 33 grams of fat! My fears were confirmed.

Maybe they won't taste as good as they look, I hoped. After all, how good could something called a "*pili* nut" be? I unscrewed the lid and as I did, a wonderful, sweet, nutty aroma wafted up my nose and made my mouth water. I prayed they wouldn't taste as good as they smelled. I put a golden cluster of the nuts into my mouth and thought, hah! Just as I suspected—heaven, sheer, fat-laden, calorie-counting, nut heaven.

It took all my willpower to resist eating the entire contents right then and there. The only thing that stopped me was calculating the number of miles I'd have to log on the treadmill to pay for my indulgence. When I reluctantly put the container down on the kitchen counter, it seemed to whisper, "Eat me. Eat me." I admit I was tempted, but afraid if I did, like Alice, I'd grow and grow.

All through dinner, I thought about how I was going to get rid of the nuts without hurting my husband's feelings or gaining ten pounds. And, after forty years of marriage I know that when your husband gives you a gift, you wear it, dab it behind your ears, drink it or eat it or else you might not ever get another gift. I thought about eating just one a day, but knew that once I opened the container, I would eat the whole thing. I thought about throwing them out but I was afraid that if they disappeared too quickly, my husband would think I loved them so much, he'd buy me more. Just as I finished dinner, which consisted of a salad with no dressing, an apple, and four ounces of fat-free protein, the phone rang.

"Hi Lois, it's Susan. You busy tonight? Can

we come over for coffee and—?"

"Sure," I said. "See you soon." And as luck would have it, we had coffee but no "and." It was Friday and the cupboards were bare—no biscotti, no veggie chips, no pretzels, no low-cal yogurt dip. We were tapped out.

"Michael," I said, "we have nothing to go with the coffee. I know they're a gift but would you mind if I put out those wonderful *pili* nuts?"

"Fine," he said.

And so, the nuts became a snack for our unsuspecting company.

"Here, taste these," I said to Susan and Jack. "They're *pili* nuts from the Philippines. They're like pecans only lighter and crispier and covered with a glaze."

I stationed myself at the other end of the table so I wouldn't smell the aroma and be tempted to eat just one, which I knew I couldn't do. Susan and Jack tasted them and to no surprise, they ate and ate. Even Michael ate them and by the time the evening was over, only a few morsels remained.

Before going to bed, I placed the left-over nuts way in the back of a cabinet and barricaded them with a five pound bag of sugar, a two pound bag of flour and a large super-sized can of olive oil. I was pleased with myself. My willpower and ingenuity had won.

The next evening when Michael came home from work, I asked him, "Eat any chopped goat's lungs today?"

"No," he said, "but I did bring you another present."

"More nuts?" I asked apprehensively.

"Oh no," he said, "no nuts. But I did stop off and get you some Entenmann's chocolate covered doughnuts, your favorite."

Trying on Bathing Suits

Childish

Betty Crocker® is my friend and so is the Pillsbury Doughboy™. I know that in times of need, like cooking for a potluck supper, preparing an impromptu lunch for friends or bringing a snack for our weekly Scrabble game, my friends are just a shelf away. They have stood by me for years, providing dozens of cupcakes for children's birthday parties, a myriad of cookies for bake sales, and numerous desserts for those dreaded PTA meetings.

Those trusty boxes of pre-measured ingredients with their careful and simple directions have allowed me to feel like I've made something from scratch instead of having to buy from the A&P or Connie's Neighborhood Bakery.

My neighbors—gourmet cooks and master chefs—whisk, whip, fold and mold to create perfect petit fours and elegant éclairs to tempt even the most reluctant members of the Cub Scout's Fund Raising Committee. I, however, simply open a box, mix the contents with a large Grade-A egg and beat for fifty strokes. I know it's not gourmet, but it is edible and we haven't lost a committee member yet.

Still, part of me would like to be just like Julia Child. I would love to be able to whip up a frothy little confection that everyone would ooh and ah over. I'm just not a great baker or cook, nor do I have the patience or the right equipment. Having the right tools can make all the difference.

I dauntingly leaf through the Williams-Sonoma catalog. Maybe if I had brioche molds or Madeleine pans, it would be different. Maybe if I owned some of those shiny anodized tapas pans, I'd be preparing individual paellas and frittatas, too. Maybe if I owned one of those double mezzalunas, I'd be chopping my way into Italian cooking in no time. That's it! I just don't have the right equipment to be a master chef.

And then it happened! I became the owner of ramekins. Yes, ramekins, those little ceramic dishes used to bake individual quiches or *crème brulé*. Just their name evokes the aroma of thick custardy desserts and chefs dressed in starched white coats wearing tall white toques. No self-respecting gourmet chef would be caught dead in a kitchen without Wustof™ knives, a Viking stove, fresh chervil (whatever that is!) or ramekins. And now they were mine!

Actually, I inherited them. They appeared as we were going through my husband's deceased aunt's belongings.

"Do you want to keep these funny little dishes?" Michael asked as he rummaged through Aunt Estelle's kitchen cabinets.

"Are they ramekins?" I asked with eager anticipation.

"What are ramekins?" he responded.

"Are they little, white ceramic dishes with fluted lines up the sides?" I yelled from the living room.

"What kind of lines?" he asked.

"Never mind, I'll be right there," I said.

And there they were: ramekins! I ran my fingers across the edges. I imagined them in my oven filled with tasty homemade treats. Holding them in my hands, I felt downright Julia Childish. I pictured myself baking individual Quiche Lorraines, concocting marvelous single servings of caramel crusted flan, and impressing my friends with home baked egg custard like mother used to make. "Yes," I would say as I entered the room with my gastronomic feats, "Just a little something I whipped up in my ramekins."

So we wrapped those little dishes and carefully toted them home. They were my ticket into the culinary arts, my tiny step toward *chefdom,* and my first step toward independence from Betty Crocker and the Doughboy.

I immediately leafed through cookbooks looking for recipes that would put my new dishes to good use. I found some great ones from Julia. Soon my recipe box was filled with instructions on how to make milk chocolate *pots de crème,* lemon *panna cotta,* cherry almond brickle and little lime soufflés. I even went so far as to buy ingredients like heavy cream and lemon curd, but they went bad before I got a chance to use them.

Eventually, I did use those ramekins. I used them to heat up last night's leftover peas. I used them to hold Bobby Flay's steak sauce at a barbecue and I used them to hold the chocolate chips that I folded into Betty Crocker's golden yellow cake mix. I even used them to hold paper clips on my desk. Just don't tell Julia!

Potted

I love flowers, but they don't love me. They know my deep, dark secret—while other people have green thumbs, I'm all thumbs when it comes to planting or maintaining bulbs, bushes, flowers or trees.

My affliction began in elementary school ... first grade to be exact. Every year, the Brooklyn Botanical Garden sent home a checklist of seed packets for school children to order. Every year, I delighted in sitting down with my father at the kitchen table and choosing between nasturtiums, marigolds, sweet peas and asters.

Several months later, the seeds were delivered to the school packed in tiny manila envelopes with planting instructions printed on them. Like the rest of my classmates, I made a planter from my milk container saved from snack time. I filled it with potting soil provided by my teacher, Mrs. Schwartz. I painstakingly put in several tiny marigold seeds, watered them, put them in the sun and waited ... and waited ... and waited.

In the meantime, wanting to get the most out of this educational experience, Mrs. Schwartz made a bar graph out of oak tag to chart our botanical progress. Down the left side were the names of the students and across the top was the growth of the plants noted in inches. We carefully charted our progress and after several weeks Alan Birnbaum's aster had grown two inches, Karen Klein's nasturtium had grown three and just about everyone else's had at least a few tiny green shoots stretching out toward the sun. Everyone, that is, except me—no inches, no little green shoots, no progress, no little bar on my part of the graph. This experience was repeated many times during my elementary school days, so when it came time to write the inevitable "What I Want to be When I Grow Up" essay, I wasn't going to choose horticulturist or landscaper.

Years later, when I became a school teacher, a student gave me a wonderful "hens and chicks" plant that was so symbolic of my relationship with my class. But even though I nurtured, watered and tended to its every need, it died an untimely death.

Maybe because I grew up in the city, where

blooming shrubbery and dazzling annuals were so rare, I never learned to plant things properly. Surrounded by cement instead of soil, I never established a good rapport with trees, flowers and bushes. My Christmas cactus never blooms at Yule time and the purple lilacs I planted in my backyard turned out not to be purple at all, but white. The amaryllis bulb my sister-in-law gave me for my birthday strained to produce one meager bloom, even though I followed the directions meticulously. My Japanese red maple looks like it is about to return to its native land any day now. I have forlorn forsythia, seedy looking sedums and wretched rhododendrons. Violets shrink from my touch and dogwood trees bark at me, warning me to keep away ... far, far away.

In desperation, I've even tried talking to my plants and they've talked back to me. They don't use words of course, but their actions speak for themselves. My Peace Lily seems to be at war with my watering schedule—its leaves are dropping and it no longer produces those delicate papery white flowers I love. My snake plant hisses when I pass by and my pots of Wandering Jew look like they're headed for the Dead Sea.

I finally decided to replace the live plants

with dried sprigs, plastic petals and silken blooms that only require a light dusting. I've stopped trying to make things in my garden grow and I rely on a landscaper to plant greenery in my yard that needs little or no care from me. And this spring, I vowed not to plant any flowers at all, preferring instead to gaze upon the beautiful flora in my neighbor's yard.

I have steadfastly resisted purchasing the velvety blue and yellow pansies that beckoned to me from in front of the supermarket. I stopped myself from putting seed packets into my shopping cart and I threw out all the gardening catalogs that filled my mailbox. Into the recycle bin went Burpees®, Jackson and Perkins®, and Smith and Hawken®. And I drove quickly past Frank's Nursery, Whispering Pines and Bob's Flower Shop so I wouldn't even be tempted. But, it was all for nothing.

"Hi, Lois," my friend Pat said, as she entered my house with several flats of pansies. "I picked up a few for myself and thought they'd look great in your yard, too."

"Thank you, they're gorgeous," I said with as upbeat a voice as I could muster. I looked at the flowers and hoped they hadn't heard about my poor track record. As I marveled at their beautiful petals, I thought that maybe this time would be different ... maybe this time they would grow and prosper under my supervision. Just maybe this spring I would have flowers in my garden that would put my neighbor's to shame. I even picked up the plants and gently tried to reassure them by whispering, "It's okay fellas, I'll take good care of you."

I know it was just my imagination, but they seemed to whisper back, "Come on Lois, we've heard all about you and know that no matter what you do, no matter how hard you try, we're all still going to pot."

Trying on Bathing Suits

Leaf Me Alone

It is the classic autumnal serenade—a cacophony of leaf blowers accompanied by the scritch, scritch, scratch of rakes across leaf strewn lawns. It's when the beautiful leaves that once gave us pleasure and shade, suddenly turn against us, becoming a challenge and chore. Yes, when fall comes to the northeast, it's time to get out of the easy chair, turn off the football game and do battle with nature.

Everyone seems to have his own method of dealing with the onslaught of fall foliage. Our young, energetic neighbor, Brian, has been out blowing his leaves into the woods every Saturday morning at 10 AM since the beginning of October. He wears protective earmuffs to prevent hearing loss, but unfortunately, they don't muffle the sound for us—the people next door who enjoy sleeping in on weekend mornings. As soon as we hear the trumpeting noise from Brian's blower, my husband, a veteran leaf battler, covers his head with a pillow and mutters and mumbles to himself. I'm glad the pillow mutes his words, since I'm sure none of them contain more than four letters. He reluctantly gets out of bed and hollers to me over the sound of Brian and His-Amazing-Leaf-Blower.

"Doesn't he know that lifting a rake or starting a leaf blower until every leaf has fallen off every tree is a waste of time and energy?" he asks.

Michael not only waits until our maples, oaks and dogwoods are totally bare, but until our neighbors' trees are leafless, too. He's not going to clean up our lawn only to have it marred by an errant leaf from a nearby yard. By the time he blows and rakes, the once cherry red Japanese maple leaves and the maroon dogwood leaves are extra crispy and brown. They snap, crackle and pop under our feet. As we laboriously sweep them onto a blue tarp, Michael starts to grumble again, only now there are no pillows to muffle his words.

"Michael," I say to him, "I don't know why you're so upset. Just a few months ago I suggested we move to Arizona or Florida and it was you who said, "But, I'd miss the change of seasons."

His grumbling stops, replaced by a sudden

spurt of energy that whips the leaves into a frenzy. The November wind swirls the leaves round and round and they scamper across our neighborhood like mice. Squirrels romp on them, dogs run through them, as the rest of our neighbors contemplate how to get rid of them, each in their own way.

Steve, a veteran of many leaf-laden autumns in the north, has given up trying to take on this task by himself. His sons, who once helped him rake and bag, have grown up, moved out and now have leaf problems of their own. These days, Steve sits in his den reading his law books, occasionally glancing out the window to see how much progress his gardeners have made clearing his lawn of fall debris. He contentedly watches as the autumn leaves drift by his window—those autumn leaves of red and gold that are swiftly raked and bagged, thankfully, by someone else. He's pleased that the only effort he has exerted this fall is writing a check to his clean-up crew.

John, our neighbor across the street, blew his leaves into the road and waited too long to bag them. He never did that again. The next morning, a mischievous fall wind blew them back into his yard. Now, John carefully packages his leaves in environmentally acceptable, biodegradable brown paper bags. They stand in neat rows at the curb waiting to be collected by the town's Department of Conservation.

By Thanksgiving, all the leaves in our neighborhood have been removed to the woods, mulched, or bagged, except for Bill's. Bill is our devil-may-care neighbor around the block who doesn't seem to notice that the tree holding his hammock no longer provides any shade. He doesn't mind that his summer garden, once resplendent with luscious red tomatoes and glossy green zucchini now bears a crop of dry leaves. He doesn't care that his barbecue and lawn furniture are covered with foliage and a mound of leaves has collected at his front door.

I pass Bill's yard each day. Just what is his master plan and what is he waiting for? I drive by each morning and see that not one leaf has been removed. I'm perplexed by Bill's lack of fall spirit or maybe I'm jealous because he doesn't have any blisters on his hands from raking like I do. One morning I wave hello to him and say, "Nice crop of leaves this year, Bill." No response from him, just a smile as he takes a drag of his pipe. That afternoon, a sign appears on Bill's fence that explains it all, "Free leaves," it says. "You rake 'em, you take 'em and coming soon, free snow."

No Sale

I just can't resist a sale, a bargain, or a deal. A 50% discount gives me goose bumps. Clearance racks lure me with their promise of great buys at reduced prices and a buy-one-get-one-free offer seduces my credit cards right out of their little plastic pockets in my wallet.

January is a bargain hunter's delight. That's the time of year when all those who revel in red dot specials come together to find the holy grail of shopping—that 'must have' item at a ridiculously low price. That's the time of year when the 'After Christmas Sale' meets 'The End of Season Sale' and bisects the 'January White Sales'. I get tingly all over just thinking about it.

I set out last week on my first bargain-hunting soiree of the season, armed with those necessary tools of the shoppers' trade: coupons, coupons, coupons. Carefully clipped from the newspaper or received in the mail as a reward for my patronage, they provided me with an opportunity to take those sale prices down to a new level. The words on the coupons, "winter sale and clearance", "all day savings pass", and "storewide savings", burned a hole in my pocket and put a lilt into my step. One department store had valued my business so much that it even sent me a special $5.00-off certificate. I didn't know which department to hit first—the linen department to buy those plush Royal Velvet® towels for the hall bathroom; the shoe department for The Easy Spirit® walking shoes that I so desperately needed after downing all those holiday goodies; or the Ladies' Wear for that fluffy little cashmere sweater I had eyed months before when it was full price.

Cleanliness being next to godliness, I decided to buy the Royal Velvet first. The moss green, toasted almond, bittersweet rose, autumn mist and peacock blue of the towels swirled in my head like a rainbow. Why did they call it a white sale when there was hardly a white towel or white sheet in the whole department? I selected six hand towels in perfect peach for my bathroom at the sale price of $4.99 each. Let's see, I said to myself, $29.94, less the 15 % off for the coupon is $25.45, less the $5.00 cash certificate came to $21.45—a real bargain! I put them on the counter and as the cashier rang them up, I visualized them with the peach, pale green and white wallpaper of my powder room. My, I thought, they would be a beautiful match, so soft and absorbent too.

"That'll be $29.94," the cashier said.

"Wait a minute," I said, "What about the coupon and the certificate?"

"I'm sorry ma'am," she said, "But the coupon isn't valid for Royal Velvet and the cash certificate can't be used in this department."

I looked at her in disbelief and then eyeballed the coupon. At first, I couldn't see the disclaimer, but upon putting on my reading glasses, I saw it down the left side in print so small it could have been an insurance policy. There in the tiniest letters it read: excludes designers, collections and specials. Okay, I thought, there must be other things I can buy with these, but upon further examination of the coupons, I realized my options were extremely limited.

Below the large letters that screamed *Use your savings pass over and over again*, there was smaller print ... much smaller print ... that enumerated these exclusions: Not to be used for cashmere (there went my sweater), cosmetics, fragrances, designer handbags, maternity, electronic equipment, phones, vacuums, furniture, mattresses, food and candy, regularly priced Liz Claiborne®, Ralph Lauren®, Tommy Hilfiger®, DKNY®, and Easy Spirit (there went my shoes). They were also not to be used for watches, crystal, china, Godiva®, Waterford®, Levis® and Kenneth Cole®. And to top it all off, it was not valid on specials, super buys, best values, price breaks, prior purchases, services, gift certificates or clearance center purchases.

Undaunted by these limitations, I set out to find something in the store, anything, that would satisfy my hunger for a bargain and allow me to partake in this spectacular coupon opportunity. After many hours of traipsing through the store, looking at racks and racks of clothing, shelves of picked over accessories and no-name pots and pans, I finally found something of value that would warrant using my precious coupons.

Over in the corner, on the first floor, shoved behind a rack of Calvin Klein® jeans at full price, of course, was a rack of winter scarves. With big, bold, red and white stripes, they would be suitable for The Cat in The Hat. Not exactly my style, but they would certainly keep me warm. Overjoyed at my find, I took out my credit card and reveled at the thought of finally being able to use it. But, before I did, I noticed some fine print on the sign above the scarves. This time I didn't bother to put on my glasses. I could guess what it said: This item can only be bought by customers who were born under a blue moon, in a leap year, and who can hop on one foot with one hand tied behind their back while whistling "Dixie."

I put away my credit card, put the coupons in the trash and headed home empty-handed and defeated. My husband, Michael, greeted me at the door. Seeing my weary face he said, "Well, you certainly don't look happy. Bad day?"

"Sort of," I replied.

"I know just the thing to perk you up a bit," Michael said. "Let's go out to dinner. I have a two-for-one coupon for Rainbow Wok."

Trying on Bathing Suits

Basic Training

It's the quest of everyone who rides the commuter rails—a seat in which to contemplate the day ahead, a place to lay your hat and a resting place for your rear.

"You think we'll get a seat on this one?" I asked my husband Michael, a veteran commuter and Metro North Maven, as we stood on the platform waiting for the southbound 7:52 express. "I really don't want to stand all the way into Manhattan. I've got a full day of shopping ahead of me."

"Just stay close to me," he said. "After over 30 years of commuting, I've got it down to a science."

As the train pulled into the station, we were pushed forward by the throng of commuters clambering to get aboard. I held onto Michael's arm for dear life as we entered the train. He quickly assessed the available seating.

"Not this car," he said as he barreled toward the next one dragging me with him.

"What? Why not?" I asked noticing many available seats.

"All the two-seaters are gone and the people in the three-seaters in this car are *leaners*," he said.

"What?"

"Leaners, tall men," he said. "When they fall asleep, they tend to lean—nothing like having a six footer leaning on you all the way into Manhattan."

Michael maneuvered us toward the big heavy doors that read "No riding between the cars." As I precariously crossed the treacherous threshold into the next car, he turned to me and said, "Look for petite women. If we have to share a three-seater, at least they won't take up much room. Find someone not reading the New York Times or working on a laptop since they tend to spread out. And, at all costs, avoid anyone on a cell phone!"

I saw her as soon as we entered the next car. She was a petite blond about five feet tall not weighing more than 100 pounds. No laptop, no unwieldy New York Times to spread out, no big attaché case loaded with papers to work on and no cell phone—just a tiny Coach purse and a copy of Vanity Fair.

"There," I said happily motioning to the

blonde. "Over there."

"Next car," he said dragging me onward racing past other commuters all in competition for the perfect seat, all spilling their morning coffee as they forged on.

"Next car? Why?" I asked, almost losing my balance as the train lurched forward and left the station.

"Didn't you notice the baby sitting behind her? No morning commuter in his right mind ever sits in a car with a baby. He'll be wailing within two minutes, cutting into my morning nap."

We moved shakily on, bouncing back and forth with the train's movements, and into the next car where we were able to find a three-seater all to ourselves. I was ecstatic thinking we had just found the Holy Grail of every veteran commuter. Just as I was ready to settle in, Michael pulled out a piece of black paper and a roll of tape from his attaché case. He leaned over and attached the paper to the window as I looked on in amazement.

"We're seated on the wrong side of the river with the sun coming in from the east. After shopping, when you get on the train sit on the side without the sun and remember, don't take a local, they stop at every town," he said. My lesson in commuting over, he sat back, put in his earplugs and closed his eyes for the next 45 minutes.

As if on cue, he woke up five minutes before we arrived at Grand Central Station.

"Quick," he said, "grab your things and make your way to the doors. It's the only way to avoid the crowd." A few minutes later, we exited the train.

"Have a great day shopping," Michael said as he kissed me goodbye. And I did.

I hit Macy®, West Elm® and The Gap®. I was bedazzled by Bendel®, tantalized by Tiffany® and lured in by Louis Vuitton. I shopped until I dropped and before I knew it, it was 4 o'clock and time to head home. Glancing at my train schedule, I noticed there was an express at 4:12 or a local at 4:20. If I ran all the way, I could make the express. Huffing and puffing and laden down with shopping bags, I made it onto the 4:12 just before the doors closed. I was pleased with myself until I looked around and realized there were no seats available.

I moved on to the next car with no luck—every seat was taken. I moved on and on through all the doors until the last car. At the very end was a single window seat next to tall man. He had copies of The New York Times, The Wall

Street Journal and the latest Time magazine on a pile next to him. The seat directly in front of him was occupied by an important looking businessman in a pinstriped suit deep in a cell phone conversation with his wife. "You know I don't like Jarlsburg," he said, "get the domestic Swiss instead." And sitting directly in back of the tall man was a woman with a squirming baby.

Undaunted, I approached the seat and asked the man with all the reading material, "Sir, would you mind moving those over?" Reluctantly, he gathered his things and let me sit down. As the train moved out of Grand Central, the afternoon sun streamed through the window. I reached down into one of my shopping bags and pulled out a plastic bag from CVS®. I removed a pack of construction paper, took out a black piece and taped it to the window. I put my new pair of earplugs into my ears and prepared for a nice 45-minute nap. But before I closed my eyes, I looked over at my 6-foot-tall seatmate and prayed he wasn't a leaner.

Trying on Bathing Suits

It's the time of year that every woman dreads. It's more painful than childbirth and more daunting than making dinner for your mother-in-law for the first time. It's that time of year when you regret having had that second piece of sweet potato pie on Thanksgiving, downing all those shrimp puffs on New Year's Eve and eating that whole box of Godivas™ on Valentine's Day—even though you meant to eat just one.

It's that time of year when I, like so many other women, rue the day I let my membership to the fitness club lapse and therefore not doing enough squat thrusts, mini crunches and bicep curls to tone up my body. Yes, it's that time of year when bathing suits insidiously appear in stores all over the country, making grown women feel inadequate, or maybe too adequate.

This year, I am determined to find the perfect suit, one that will hide my thighs, obliterate my abdomen and beautify my bottom. I've done my homework by reading all the fashion magazines in my doctor's office. I know that small-busted women should wear halters, shirred tops or suits with push-up bras, while large-bosomed women need a high neckline to de-emphasize the bust line. A black bottom and a print top will disguise a bottom-heavy figure and diagonal blocks of color will draw attention away from a thick waist. And last but not least, the *fashionistas*, in their infinite wisdom, have declared black, the "new black" for this swim season.

Armed with all this knowledge, I walk through the mall on my quest to find a flattering suit. I stop to hiss at the new *Sports Illustrated* swimsuit issue prominently displayed in the bookstore. I remember how much I hate Bar Refaeli and look for evidence of air brushing. But even as I do, I regret taking that advanced *feng shui* course at the local high school instead of the high impact aerobic dance class.

I make my way to the swimsuit department and find myself in the midst of bikinis, tankinis, bandinis, camikinis (whatever they are), maillots and sarongs. I take an armful in varying sizes into the fitting room. I don't like the name "fitting room" since rarely do I find anything that fits. I've selected a number of suits with those little boy legs that are supposed to disguise

Trying on Bathing Suits

flabby thighs, but when I try them on I think that the only ones who would look good in this style is little boys. I try on one of those suits with the little skirt on the bottom. I twist and turn in the mirror to get a good view from all angles. The suit really speaks to me. It says, "Yes, you've overindulged. Yes, you've under exercised and now you have to wear this stupid looking suit with the skirt as penance."

Okay, no little boy legs and no skirts. Next, I try on one of those suits with the tummy control panel guaranteed to make you look at least five pounds thinner. Amazingly, it does. The only problem is where those five pounds have gone. I can't breathe. Not only can't I breathe, I can't sit or walk either. Those five pounds are now squashing my internal organs so badly that they are all screaming in pain. I tug and I pull and I tug and I pull some more, but just like a boa constrictor, the suit tightens its hold. It takes me ten whole minutes to wrest this lethal little piece of Lycra® off of me. I sit down on the bench to rest and take big gulping breaths for a few minutes.

Resuscitated, I try a high-cut number that is supposed to make my legs look longer. It really doesn't. Maybe, I think, I'm standing too close. Maybe, I need to see it in a different light. I move out of the dressing room to the common area to get a better look and a new prospective. Just then, a young girl no older than fourteen and so thin that she couldn't get a needle on a scale to move, comes out too. She has no thighs, no butt, no abdomen and no breasts. She's wearing an itsy-bitsy, teeny-weeny, hardly-even-there bikini. She turns to her friend and asks, "Do you think this suit makes me look fat?" I want to take her by the throat and force feed her like they do to those ducks they use for *foie gras*. I want to slap some Twinkies on her thighs, some mashed potatoes around her waist and some Hagan-Daas on her bottom.

What is she thinking? I ask myself while looking at this anorexic young girl. Wait a minute, what am I thinking? I go back into the fitting room and try on a simple suit with normal cut legs, no tummy control panel, no skirt or shirring. I twist and turn to see myself from every angle.

My tummy sticks out a little (okay, maybe more than a little), my thighs look just a bit flabby and my butt, well, let's just leave it at that. I like it! I really like it. It's me. This suit makes a statement. It says:

"I've had two children and I'm proud. I really, really love Godiva chocolates and don't like sit-ups."

The only concession I've made is the color. It's black, the "new black." The *fashionistas* would be proud.

Trying on Bathing Suits

Final Resting Place

I am afraid to die. Oh, I know it is as inevitable as the period at the end of this sentence, the amen after a prayer, and Pepto-Bismol™ after a pepperoni-sausage-anchovy pizza. I know that from dust we are and from dust we must return, but it's where my dust will be lying for eternity that worries me.

Years ago, my father offered my husband and me a great deal on burial plots.

"Listen," he said, "The Wolkewisker Society has lots of plots available at Beth David Cemetery. They're practically giving them away. I'll get you two."

This was a topic that I tried not to think about. Frankly, the thought of being in the ground surrounded by worms didn't hold much appeal for me. I considered thinking out of the box.

"Ever hear of cryogenics?" I asked my father.

"What?" he said incredulously.

"Never mind," I said.

"So," my father asked, "what do you think about the cemetery plots?"

I didn't know what to think. I was young and relatively healthy and any thoughts I entertained about going underground those days involved taking the subway to Macy's.

"I'll have to think about it," I said.

"Okay, but listen," my father said, "you'll be surrounded by your loving family. You will be near me and your mother."

Nothing like throwing in a little guilt! But actually, the more I considered it, the more sense it made to be interred in the family plot in Belmont, Queens.

The Wolkewisker Society, a holdover from the old burial societies in Poland, had chosen their sacred burial ground next to Belmont Racetrack. At least they would have something fun to do, that is if they ever stopped fighting and complaining. Knowing my relatives, I would bet money that they were passing up those trifectas for much more personal diversion. I am sure that Aunt Rachel is still screaming at her brother Sammy for giving her a second hand silver tray for her birthday. Bought at one of the shops on the lower East Side, it was thoughtfully engraved: To Esther and Harry on their 20th anniversary. I am sure that my Aunt Anna is still bossing around her poor husband Irving, and that my grandfather is still wondering why he couldn't take his money with him.

Beth David is a very old cemetery. Its lanes are barely wide enough for one car to pass through. On Machpeliah Street, an old black wrought iron gate creaks open to reveal the family burial ground consisting of narrow rows of etched , slate gray stones. Although many of them have round blue stickers in the left hand corner indicating that the plots have perpetual care, most of the graves are unkempt and overgrown. Once a year I come to pull the weeds, trim the branches and tidy up around the graves of my beloved family members. It's both comforting and heart wrenching to pass the loving mothers, devoted fathers, brothers, sisters, aunts and uncles in my family tree.

It's also sobering to think that one day I will join them. I wonder who will trim and weed and plant ivy for me? More importantly, next to whom will I be buried? The graves adjacent to my parents are already taken. Will I be buried next to my cousin Elaine who I haven't spoken to in thirty years? Will I be buried next to my Uncle Abraham? He wasn't much of a talker in life so I doubt he'll be too chatty in death. Will I be buried next to Uncle Murray and have to inhale his cigar smoke for eternity? Or will I be buried next to my grandfather and have to listen to him poring over his old bank books?

Despite my father's generous offer, my husband wants to turn it down.

"I always thought we would be buried together in my family plot," he said.

The Podoshen Family is buried in Mt. Moriah Cemetery in New Jersey. I must admit it's far more attractive and spacious than Beth David. The graves are on a pleasant hillside and are very well kept. Of course, there is no racetrack there but I'm sure the residents have all found something to occupy their time.

"Is there room for me?" I ask Michael.

"Yes," he said, "and I have all the deeds. You can pick whichever grave you want."

Like any prospective homeowner, I look the plots over carefully. There's a space next to Michael's Aunt Charlotte, but I'm going to pass on that one. I'm convinced that she has been buried upside down, with her feet where her head should be. Maybe her dearly departed husband who is buried on her other side doesn't mind, but I don't want to spend eternity with her size eights in my face.

I walk through the graveyard assessing the other possibilities. The spot next to Cousin

Bernie is vacant. That might be interesting since he was once a theater critic and knew people like La Liz and Ali McGraw.

The spot next to Uncle Morris is available, too. The two of us could reminisce about the good old days in Brooklyn; about corner grocery stores, penny candy and Coney Island. And the plot next to Aunt Estelle, who was once a Rockette, could be mine just for the asking. "My father thought only loose women went on stage in those days," she told me before she passed away. "He dragged me home after a week."

I know choosing Mt. Moriah will make my husband happy and I have a good feeling about my ultimate decision to be buried there, until we get home.

"Michael," I ask. "Who else will be buried in those plots that you have the deeds to?"

"Well," he says, "My mother, my sister and my cousins Ann and Deane. Oh, and of course, there's one for Lenny."

Sheer terror sweeps over me. How could I have forgotten? The women in the family have dubbed him "Lenny the Letch." Married to Michael's deceased cousin Susan, he is always on the prowl. He alone is responsible for the dress code now in effect for all women attending any wedding, bar mitzvah or graduation party. He is the reason there are no backless dresses, no strapless gowns or halters at the Podoshen affairs these days. Cousin Lenny has a habit of rubbing his beard on any exposed female skin causing both humiliation and burns. And when he isn't rubbing his beard on us, other parts are busy at work. The last thing I need is to spend eternity with Lenny jumping my bones!

"Swear," I say to Michael, looking around for anything that he might consider holy or sacred. "Swear on your running shoes."

"Swear what?" he asks.

"You know what," I say. "Swear that you will not bury me next to Lenny. So help me if you do, I will come back to haunt you forever!"

"I swear," he says laughingly. "I really do."

"Okay," I say. "Then Mt. Moriah it is."

Hopefully, it will be a final resting place that I can live with.

Do, Re, Mi and DNA

Ever since I was a young child tickling the ivories of a toy instrument, I wanted to play the piano. Unfortunately, my family couldn't afford one and we didn't have room in our small Brooklyn apartment even if we could.

In elementary school, I watched as my friends took lessons in the auditorium of P.S. 226 after school. Their hands moving deftly over the keys of the old baby grand used for assemblies, school plays and to herald the winners of the perfect attendance awards. When they practiced the national anthem, however badly, they looked so important sitting straight and tall on the piano bench that I was envious.

Happily, when I was ten years old, my parents decided to round out my education with music lessons. After much deliberation, they chose an instrument compatible with my diminutive size, scrawny arms and skinny legs—the accordion! Not exactly what I had hoped for, but the accordion, with its piano-like keys, was the closest I was going to get to a baby grand.

My father always wanted the best for his children, so just any old accordion teacher wouldn't do.

"Lois," he said, "you're going to the Joe Biviano School of Music in Manhattan." This school was the crème de la crème of accordion schools in New York. Every Saturday morning, Dad packed me, my mother and younger brother into the car and headed down to the city from Brooklyn to foster my musical education. We would get out of the car in front of the school, while Dad rode round and round in his prized fifty-seven Chevy until he found a parking space.

During the first session with my teacher, Mario, I was fitted for my new instrument. Mario strapped the accordion to my shoulders and watched as I almost keeled over. Like a sapling bent from the weight of a heavy, wet snow, I almost snapped in two.

"Don't worry," he said, "we'll get you one the right size."

Soon I became the owner of my very own accordion. It had smooth keys down the right-hand side, numerous buttons on the left, and a trimming of faux mother-of-pearl on either side of the bellows. I was also outfitted with a very professional-looking music stand and a thick music book.

"For this week," Mario said, "I want you to memorize the names of the notes. I'll give you a trick to help you remember them. The lines are e-g-b-d-f—**E**very **G**ood **B**oy **D**oes **F**ine. The spaces are F-A-C-E. It couldn't be easier."

Mario was right, that was easy, but actually playing the accordion wasn't.

I realize now that my lack of musical ability had to be genetic. I don't remember anyone in my family, on either side, being musical, except for my Uncle Seymour and even he wasn't all that good.

It didn't take too many lessons for me to figure out two things: one - I was naturally non-musical, and two - I hated to practice. I just wondered how long it would take my parents to reach the same conclusion.

Every afternoon I would strap on that weighty accordion and pretend to look at the music on the stand.

"Lois, are you practicing?" my mother would ask rhetorically.

"Yes, Mom," I answered, as I played a few notes. Actually, I was practicing … practicing how to tell my parents that I wasn't born to be a musician and didn't want to do this anymore only I didn't want to disappoint them. So we continued going to Manhattan every Saturday and I continued to place that albatross around my neck.

Even Mario was beginning to feel sorry for me. I could see the pity and disappointment in his eyes every time he tried to teach me a new song.

And just when I thought things couldn't get any worse, they did!

"Lois," Mario said one day, trying not to look me directly in the eyes, "the Biviano School holds a concert every year at the Barbizon Plaza Hotel. I've teamed you up with a girl your own age, Rosemarie, and you'll be playing a duet of *Clare de Lune*."

I couldn't believe what I was hearing. Bad enough that Mario and I both knew how nonmusical I was, but soon the whole world would know, too! Panic—sheer panic—ran through me. Surely my parents wouldn't do this to me, I thought, But before you could say "Lady of Spain," my mother was on the phone telling all our relatives to set aside the date. Aunt Sarah was even making me a special white organdy dress for the occasion. I was doomed. My only hope was that Rosemarie was really good and could carry me through this.

As it turned out, the kindest thing I could

say about Rosemarie's playing was that at least she didn't upstage me. No matter how hard we tried, we just couldn't master *Clare de Lune* alone ... or together. I prayed I would get sick the day of the performance, but no such luck.

The auditorium at the hotel filled to capacity with friends and relatives eager to hear the fruits of the students' efforts. My parents, grandparents, aunts and uncles were excited. As I stood looking out over the vast audience, I started to get nauseous and to top it all off, that starched organdy dress began to itch. Rosemarie didn't look like she was faring any better, but somehow, we made it through the song, even if we didn't start and finish at the same time.

To my surprise, the audience responded with a roar of applause as if we had just given them a flawless performance of Beethoven's *Fifth Symphony*. Although my parents were beaming that day, several weeks later they decided my time would be better spent pursuing something else ... anything else! My accordion was relegated to the downstairs closet where it stayed forlorn and in disgrace for years to come.

My luck decreed that I marry a man who was also musically challenged—he found out about his affliction by taking clarinet lessons. Naturally, considering our mutually deficient

DNA, we figured music lessons for our future progeny would be a waste of time.

But then our first-born son, at ten years of age, came home one day and announced, "Mrs. Gold says we can take music lessons at school this year. I signed up for viola."

I cringed and hoped that maybe our family curse didn't apply to stringed instruments.

After a few weeks of lessons, Jeff's love of the viola seemed to be waning, as did the amount of time he spent practicing.

"Jeff," I asked him, "are you practicing in there?"

"Yes, Mom," he said in that lackluster tone I could relate to so well. As his bow screeched across the strings, I just couldn't stand his pain any longer. It was time to come clean.

"Jeff," I said as I tenderly put my arm around him, "it's not your fault, it's your DNA, our DNA really, it's missing the musical gene."

He hugged me and smiled with relief. And so, his viola joined my accordion in exile.

Several years later, our younger son, Lawrence, approached us at the dinner table with a request. "Mom, Dad," he said, "I would like to take guitar lessons. I really, really want to do this, can I, please?" he implored.

I wanted to run screaming from the table,

but controlled myself.

"I don't think it's such a good idea, dear," I said.

"You let Jeff take viola. That's not fair," he said. And so, against our better judgment, we let Lawrence take guitar lessons.

Maybe it was because he was conceived in a house so close to a nuclear power plant, but Lawrence seemed to have a mutant gene. He could not only play the guitar, but he was good, very good—actually talented. And he loved to practice, day and night. In no time at all, he was playing riffs from songs by Eric Clapton and Chuck Berry and jamming on 12-bar blues.

One day as he picked up his guitar to practice, he turned to me and asked, "Any requests, Mom?"

"*Clare de Lune*," I said, "Please, play *Clare de Lune*."

Chicken Soup in August

There is nothing worse than being home with a sick child, unless, of course, it's being home with a sick husband. One stormy Thursday, the skies threatened to open up any minute and spew torrents of rain. The wind was whipping the trees into a frenzy, but they weren't the only things in turmoil that day.

"I don't think you should go to Rhode Island feeling like this," I said to my husband, as he got ready for an overnight business trip. "I really don't like the sound of your cough."

"It's just a summer cold or some kind of 24-hour bug. I've just got a little chill. I'll be fine," he said, exhibiting the common male reaction to illness.

"A chill in August is not a little thing. You're sick and there's a storm brewing. Just cancel the meeting and stay home," I implored.

"Can't," he said as he picked up his briefcase and walked toward the door. "I'll call you tomorrow."

When the phone rang the next day, I could have predicted the conversation.

"I made it here all right but I got drenched last night. My cough is worse and I'm sweating a lot. The meeting is over and I'm heading home now," he said.

"Be careful," I replied.

By the time he arrived home, three and a half hours later, his face was gray—grayer than day old hamburger, grayer than a February sky, grayer than the silvery hairs that were suddenly appearing on my head. He shivered and coughed as I helped him off with his jacket. It was a deep hacking cough, a "go to the doctor" cough, an "I need medication" cough.

"Michael, you need to go to the doctor," I said. But in my heart I knew getting him to go to the doctor was going to be about as easy as getting a man, any man, to ask directions when he's lost—genetically impossible!

"Why?" he asked almost innocently.

"Oh, I don't know, maybe because she has a degree in medicine, can diagnose illnesses, can use a stethoscope to listen to your lungs and write prescriptions," I said.

"I just have a summer cold, that's all. It will go away in seven days if I ignore it and in a week if I go to the doctor," he said emphatically.

"Very funny," I said worried about how he looked and sounded. Over the weekend the cough got worse, his temperature escalated and he spent most of his time in bed, sweating. His eyes were dull with circles under them, the cough was deeper now and more foreboding and his skin was clammy.

I nagged him. "Go to the doctor!" I must have said it a million times that weekend.

No response.

I cajoled him. "Go to the doctor. She might even give you a lollipop if you're good boy."

No response.

"Go to the doctor, please? Pretty, please?"

No response. No response until Tuesday morning.

"I think I need to go to the doctor," Michael said between coughs. "My temperature just isn't going down."

No response from me—just a glare.

After spending several hours in the doctor's waiting room, it took exactly a nanosecond for her to diagnose his illness—pneumonia. She prescribed an antibiotic and bed rest.

"Get a chest x-ray, come back to see me on Friday and do not go to work this week," she told him.

The antibiotic and chest x-ray were one

thing, but the bed rest and staying home was another. Michael is the classic type "A" personality—actually a triple "A" personality. He simply can't sit still. He gets up at 5 every morning to run four miles. He took up skiing at the age of forty and roller blading at fifty. The last time he stayed home for a week was in fifth grade when he had the measles.

His cough was so bad, he moved out of our room into the room vacated by our son. There, amid the baseball card collection and Star Wars figures, he took his temperature so many times hoping that it would read 98.6, I was afraid he was going to get mercury poisoning.

He didn't look like he was going to get better anytime soon, so I called my sister.

"Hi Paula," I said. "We'll have to take a rain check for Saturday night. Michael has pneumonia."

"Pneumonia in August?"

"Yes, and he's driving me crazy!"

"Go to the video store and get him some movies."

"He said he doesn't have the patience," I replied.

"Books! Go to the library and get him some books," she suggested.

"He says he has no patience for that either."

"Just sit him in front of the television and give him the remote—that's what I do with Howie."

"Tried it," I said. "Michael says that there are 500 stations and nothing of any interest to watch. And he just hates Jerry Springer."

"Well," said Paula, "there's only one thing left to do."

"What's that?"

"Take two valium and call me in the morning!"

The next day I called all our friends to tell them the news. Their reactions were all the same.

"He didn't go to the doctor until Tuesday?" I could hear the accusatory tone in their voices, as if I had been derelict in my wifely duties. I could almost see the looks of disdain and disappointment in their faces.

"I tried to make him go. I really did," I told them all. "He's a grown man for goodness sake. He's fifty-five, not five. I can't make him do anything he doesn't want to do." This was followed by silence on the other end of the line, which I interpreted to mean that I just hadn't tried hard enough. I got off the phone and did the only other thing I knew how to do in situations like this—make a steaming pot of chicken soup, even though it was August.

Bowls of the golden elixir were followed by a rousing game of Scrabble. I knew when he started making words like "depression," "boredom," and "monotonous," the game was over and I had lost.

While Michael started to get ready for bed that evening, I planned the activities for the next few days. Scrabble™ would be replaced by gin rummy and another Bruce Willis movie. Gin rummy would then be replaced by double solitaire. After Bruce Willis, we might move on to Schwarzenegger. By the end of the week, I was running out of activities and Michael was getting so bored that even Jerry Springer was looking good to him.

By the sound of Michael's cough, I knew the doctor would suggest at least another week of rest for him. I was prepared to amuse him until he was well enough to get back on his feet and become that type "A" man that I know and love. When that time came, I celebrated by putting up my feet, turning on the TV, having a little chicken soup and watching Jerry Springer.

Roll Over, Beethoven

The closest I get to classical music is listening to the Beatles' rendition of "Roll Over Beethoven." At Christmas time, I relent and listen to Tchaikovsky's *Nutcracker Suite*. But Yana, an accomplished violinist and new friend, really didn't know my taste in music yet. The invitation she sent me to attend a concert performed by the local symphony orchestra took me by surprise. I wanted to go to that concert as much as I wanted a root canal, but I didn't want to insult Yana either.

"Please come," she said when she called me that evening. "Bring your husband and your friends. It's free and it's a wonderful program. We've practiced so hard."

"Michael," I said to my husband, "Yana's invited us to a concert on December 9th."

"That's nice," he said.

"She'll be playing the violin and the program will include pieces by Beethoven, Mozart and Haydn."

"Can I bring No-Doze with me?" he asked

"Very funny," I replied. "It might be a nice change of pace and besides I don't want to disappoint her."

"Fine," he said. "Maybe we do need a dose of culture. I'll go and I think I'll call Ben, too. It's right up his alley."

Our friend Ben is a music aficionado who spends his days and nights listening to his vast collection of operas, symphonies and concertos on his state-of-the-art sound system. He can give a dissertation about Caruso's career and knows just what year Pavarotti's voice had its best timbre. He knows all the librettos from all the famous operas and even some that aren't so famous. The mere mention of Yo Yo Ma causes his face to glow and the thought of Yitzhak Perlman gives him goose bumps. He is as at home at The Met as I am at the Rock and Roll Hall of Fame. What better person to accompany us to a symphony? What better person to tell me when the movement is over and it's time to clap?

"Ben," I say when he picks up the phone. "It's Lois. I just called to make you an offer you just can't refuse. My friend Yana, who plays first violin, is performing in a concert on December 9th and it's free. Want to go?"

Ben mulls this over for a few seconds.

"You're going to hear classical music?" he asks, while violins and French horns on his CD player blare in the background. "That's a first!" Cymbals crash as he asks, "What's on the program?"

"Well," I say reading from the invitation, "Mozart's overture to *The Marriage of Figaro*, Haydn's Symphony No. 99 in E-flat major and Beethoven's Violin Concerto in D Major, Opus 61." I have no idea what I'm talking about, but it sounds important and cultured.

"That's an impressive program," Ben replies. "Who's the soloist?"

"Eric Goodman."

"Humph! I've never heard of him," Ben says.

"So, you don't want to go?" I ask.

"Of course I want to go," he says, "I would never pass up a chance to hear Beethoven in concert, especially for free."

"We'll pick you up Sunday at 12:30." As I hung up, the cymbals crashed again.

A few days later, all three of us head down to the concert.

"Ben, honestly, do you think I'm going to like this?" I ask.

"Oh yes," he replies. "*The Marriage of Figaro* was Mozart's first collaboration with Lorenzo da Ponte, a brilliant librettist. It was based on the comedy *Le Mariage de Figaro* that was considered immoral and even revolutionary for its time. Mozart's opera is unsurpassed in its mix of cleverness and sense of melancholy. You'll love Haydn's Symphony No. 99, too. It beings with an *adagio* that is as exciting as it is unsettling because of its wide-ranging modulations and this feeling persists into the *vivace* of the first movement. And what can I say about Beethoven's Violin Concerto in D Major? It's the veritable gold standard of maturity for the performing violinist since it requires both technical skill and great musical sensitivity."

"Wow," I gush, all the while realizing how out of my element I am. Bowzer from Sha-Na-Na I understand, but Beethoven? However, by the time we enter the auditorium, Ben's enthusiasm has taken hold of me and I can't wait to hear the music. I also can't wait to tell my rock and roll loving friends that I actually heard an opus, that Mozart's *Marriage of Figaro* wowed me with its unsurpassed mix of cleverness and sense of melancholy and how Beethoven's violin concerto requires equal parts of technical skill and musical sensitivity.

Yana greeted us in the crisp, formal, black and white attire of a concert violinist. Her eyes sparkled but beneath it all I could sense her nervousness.

"I'm so glad you came," she said, "it'll be so nice to look across the audience and see some friendly faces."

"Yana," I said, "This is our friend Ben, a real classical music enthusiast."

"So glad to meet you," she said as she led us to seats near the stage. "I hope you enjoy the performance." And with that she stepped onto the stage and picked up her violin and bow.

The house lights started to dim as the other musicians settled into their chairs and readied their instruments. The clarinets, French horns and trumpets gleamed in the spotlights. The conductor, in his tuxedo, raised his baton as the first and second violin, the viola, and the cello players gripped their bows. The music of Mozart filled the room. Its sound was sparkling and its charm mesmerizing. I was surprised I was actually enjoying myself and as I looked over toward Michael, I saw that he was having a good time, too. We were so drawn in by Mozart's overture and Haydn's Symphony No. 99 that time flew by quickly. Before we knew it, it was time for intermission.

"Oh, Yana," I said, as we approached the stage, "that was great."

Michael and Ben nodded in agreement.

Yana carefully put down her violin and bow. "I'm glad you liked it. We perform about two times a year. The next concert will be in March when we'll be performing Gilbert and Sullivan's *The Gondoliers*. I hope you will come," she said.

We chatted until the houselights flickered.

"See you after the show," I said, as we returned to our seats.

Again the conductor raised his baton and strains of Beethoven filled the concert hall. Bows moved skillfully across taut strings. I marveled at the wonderful sound they made.

Ben was totally involved. So involved, I was sure he had closed his eyes to heighten his listening pleasure and concentrate on the music alone—to revel in the subtle nuances of the sounds and drink in the depth of the composition. But when the soloist stepped onto the stage and began playing the famed violin concerto, I heard a noise that didn't follow Beethoven's rhythmic pattern ... a noise directly in opposition to the five timpani taps that open the work, setting the pattern for the entire first movement. It was snoring, and it was coming from Ben.

He looked so peaceful that I didn't dare wake him up and besides, I didn't want to embarrass him. It was less than a snore really, just a slight whistle and didn't seem to bother the other listeners around him. So Ben slept through his beloved Beethoven, missing the technical skill and musical sensitivity of Eric Goodman, the soloist.

The finale, with its clear rhythms and dance-like accents brought the house down. Everyone clapped and clapped. All that clapping woke Ben up and he joined the standing ovation.

"So Ben," I said, "You're the expert, what did you think of the performance?"

"Well," he said, "I really didn't like the orchestra much but the soloist was really terrific!"

Trying on Bathing Suits

John Wayne to the Rescue

They are the harbingers of spring in the suburbs, ranking right up there with spotting the first robin or seeing the first crocus pop its colorful head out of the ground. To the untrained eye, they look like tiny black specks on my kitchen counter, but I know better. Those specks represent the beginning of the sacred spring pilgrimage of all the ants within a 50-mile radius through the soft moist ground and into the nooks and crannies of my house.

Year after year, my house becomes an ant convention center and each and every room is booked and crawling with conventioneers. They come in droves and run 5K races around my bathroom mirror; play hide-'n-seek on my oriental carpet; and hold a scavenger hunt in my kitchen looking for chocolate macadamia nut cookie crumbs or a slick of grease from last night's lamb chops.

I have a plan of attack. I start by washing and scrubbing all closets, cabinets and counter tops ... and still they come. I vacuum all the carpets, rugs and hardwood floors divesting them of any morsels that ants might find appealing ... and still they come. I swab my baseboards, moldings and windowsills with bleach ... and still they come. I spray with super-duper ant and roach spray, but I am the only one who falls victim to the fumes.

By the end of the week, I'm frazzled and my house is still filled with crawling interlopers who just will not go away. I want my privacy back and am now ready to take my efforts to a higher level.

I buy several of those embarrassing ant traps that I hide from view, placing one behind the garbage can, another behind my aloe vera plant and another unobtrusively behind my refrigerator. Their placement is so inconspicuous that guests in my home don't even know they're there. The problem is, the ants don't seem to know that either.

I get bolder now and put them in plain view. Pretty soon my whole house is decorated with tiny metal canisters. I try desperately to pass them off as replicas of antique snuff boxes purchased from an exclusive boutique, and I might have gotten away with it, too, if only the words "ant trap" weren't emblazoned on them in big black letters.

The ants bring in reinforcements and I do the same. I let my fingers do the walking through the Yellow Pages to find a pest control specialist—the exterminator. He arrives at my home, thankfully, in an unmarked car to prevent alerting the neighbors or the conventioneers. He swaggers into my kitchen with all the machismo of John Wayne, ready to take on my army of ants. But just like the knock in my car engine that disappears when I enter the mechanic's shop or a nagging toothache that stops throbbing as soon as I reach the dentist's office, the ants are nowhere in sight. John Wayne is undaunted because he has a trusty weapon in his leather holster to ferret out even the slipperiest foe—his industrial strength flashlight. He spotlights every crack and crevice, every orifice inside and outside my home.

"We've hit them on all fronts," he says as he heaps handfuls of ant bait outside my front and back doors and puts a sticky ant-alluring substance around my kitchen window and baseboards.

"It will take a while to work, but in a few weeks your ants will be history," he says with all the bravado of a general that has just defeated a battalion of infantrymen.

I am ecstatic, knowing that I will not wake up to ants dancing in a conga line toward my bottle of Vermont maple syrup or diving into my sugar bowl. I'm elated that the party is over and the uninvited conventioneers will finally pack their bags and go back to the soft, moist earth where they belong. As John Wayne starts down the stairs, I gratefully gush, "Thank you."

He turns and replies, "See you next spring."

Arugula

My mother always told me to eat my vegetables, but I hated them! When I refused to eat the broccoli or Brussels sprouts on my plate, she would say, "Do you know that there are children starving in China who would love to have your vegetables?"

Although I couldn't say it out loud, I always thought, *Good, give my vegetables to them*!

The mere sight of spinach made me gag and the smell of cabbage simmering on the stove made me want to hop a freighter to China myself, where I was sure I could live a life devoid of anything green and leafy.

However, while I didn't like them as a child, as an adult I've acquired quite a taste for fresh produce. Crisp snap beans are great for my casseroles; dark blue-green broccoli enriches my stir-fries; and tender baby spinach leaves top off my salads. But while I can pick out the freshest asparagus by looking at their tips, select a ripe tomato by gently squeezing it, and weed out stalky green beans, I just can't open those plastic bags provided for them at the market.

It's the most frustrating part of my grocery shopping experience. It's worse than waiting on line at the deli counter when the number machine is broken; worse than trying to find a carton of eggs where one—or two—isn't broken; and worse than trying to obtain a container of coconut crème pie yogurt that isn't outdated. I just don't understand this. I've always had good, fine-motor coordination and my dexterity has never been in question before. I can sew, crochet and deftly use a computer keyboard. Even my left-handed penmanship is legible.

Maybe that's it, I think. *Are all the bags right-handed?* On a recent grocery shopping foray, I consulted my list before walking down the dreaded produce aisle. I needed tomatoes, cucumbers and peppers. I selected the firmest peppers, without any soft spots or blemishes, in the most beautiful green color. They would be perfect for the salad I had planned for that evening.

I ripped off a plastic bag and moved my fingers back and forth against its slippery surface like a safecracker picking a lock, but no matter how many times I tried there was just no opening this bag! I pulled and I twisted. I tugged and I tore. I blew on it. I used my nails and my teeth, but the bag just wouldn't open. In desperation, I even grabbed a celery stalk, waved it over the bag and chanted, "Abracadabra, alacazam!" But nothing would make those two thin layers of plastic obey me. On the verge of having to go down the health and beauty aids aisle for some antacid, I gave up on salad as a first course for my dinner.

As I looked around, I saw other people in the same vegetable-less position. To the right of the zucchini display stood a young woman shaking a bag to the rhythm of the music playing on the loud speaker, but even the beat of the latest Christina Aguilera song wasn't enough to part the plastic. An elderly arthritic woman looked longingly at the tomato display but knew her limitations and moved on. *Are we all on Candid Camera?* I thought, *or did Bird's Eye's frozen food division cook up this diabolic plan to increase their sales?*

Out of the corner of my eye, I saw a cart loaded down with fresh produce. There were bags of cucumbers, Harvard beets, escarole, carrots, Vidalia onions and yams. Pushing the cart was a young woman with her secret, plastic-circumventing weapon: her ten-year-old son! As she picked and chose her produce items carefully, he grabbed a bag and spat on it. As soon as he ran his fingers over the top it opened, just like magic. I should have known that no mother in her right mind would go shopping with a ten-year-old boy unless it was absolutely necessary. As clever as this method was, the spitting thing held little appeal for me. I decided that it would have to be frozen vegetables tonight after all.

As I made my way down the aisle, I noticed that the young woman at the zucchini display was still doing the plastic bag polka, without results. I figured she would be joining me at the frozen food section soon.

That night when we sat down to dinner, my husband asked," No salad?"

"Actually," I said, "a recent study by a local independent researcher has found that eating fresh vegetables can actually increase your blood pressure."

"What?" he asked incredulously.

"Oh, I just decided that frozen vegetables would be nice for a change," I said.

Luckily, he ate the frozen peas and didn't ask for a further explanation, saving me from embarrassment over my lack of prowess with pesky plastic bags. We went on this way for two whole weeks and by then I was getting pretty hungry for anything fresh, crisp and green. About that time, I ran into my friend Diane who was known for her wonderful summer salads.

"Diane," I said, "I must ask you a question about your salads."

"Oh," she replied, "everyone asks about them, the secret is buttermilk in the dressing."

"Actually what I need to know is how you get all those vegetables into the plastic bags at the market," I said.

"Oh, that! It's simple. Arugula."

"Arugula?" I asked.

"Oh yes, I always select my arugula first. The market always keeps it very moist because it wilts and dries out so quickly. I choose my arugula and while my hands are still damp, I can open five or six plastic bags with ease."

That night, salad returned to our table.

My husband was so glad to see his favorite vegetables again that he dove right in without asking any questions. After a few bites he looked up from his plate and said, "This salad is really good but there's something different about it. It has a slightly tangy taste. What is it?"

"Arugula," I said, "the secret is arugula."

It's Just a Number

As a child, I was taught never to ask a woman her age. The women in my life didn't tell the truth about it anyway. I didn't even know how old my grandmother was until her date of birth was chiseled on her tombstone and we lived together for over twenty years. Now, thanks to the information highway—and much to the chagrin of many, both young and old—no one has to ask.

A few months ago, my husband and I attended a friend's birthday party. There was sumptuous food, great wine and a tacit understanding that no one ask the guest of honor just how many candles were supposed to be on the cake. We all sang "Happy Birthday" while a solitary taper flickered on top of three tiers of chocolate sponge.

"Don't ask," whispered her husband to those in earshot, "she's very sensitive about her age."

No one asked, but when the night was over, we all rushed home to our computers. I keyed in 'zabasearch.com', put in my friend's name and state and *voilà!*—her well-kept secret a secret no more. It's just as well she only had one candle on her cake since the correct number would have lit up the Empire State Building.

Many people today don't realize how easy it is to access someone's personal information and why lying is no longer an option. My friend, Arlene, is a real gym rat and while she's happy to tell you how tight her abs are and that she has no stretch marks, she's pretty tight mouthed about her age and pretty good at stretching the truth.

"You know," she said one day after a particularly strenuous Pilates session, "I can do the downward dog, pelvic tilts and hip rolls better than women half my age!"

"Just how old are you, Arlene?" I asked, even though it went against everything I had been taught.

"I'm 52," she admitted proudly. Invigorated by the Pilates session and Arlene's uncharacteristic candor, I sprinted home. I typed "lookupanyone.com" and keyed in Arlene's full name and address. Guess what? Arlene is in pretty good shape for a woman of 52 but she's in even better shape for someone who's 62!

Lying about your age is an affliction that

isn't just relegated to women. A few years ago, our good friend, Sam, lost his beloved Faith to cancer after 42 years of wedded bliss. Distraught, he sequestered himself at home for nearly two years, eschewing any attempts to set him up with a date. Finally coming out of mourning, Sam decided to venture onto 'Match.com'. During the following months, my husband Michael received numerous emails from Sam detailing his conquests and describing all his new girlfriends.

Intrigued, Michael went to the website to look at Sam's profile.

"Lois," he said, "come in here and look at this. It's amazing. In the two years since Faith's death, Sam has miraculously gotten five years younger!"

Sam eventually got remarried to someone he met through the website and chances are she lied about her age, too.

By now, you're probably wondering how old I am and if I've ever lied about my age. When I was a teacher, my students always asked, "Mrs. Podoshen, how old are you?"

I responded with, "How old do you think I am?"

Invariably, one kind youngster said, "21?"

"Yes," I responded even if I was 31 or 41 at the time.

So, how old am I? You'll just have to go to 'lookupanyone.com' or 'zabasearch.com' to find out. And if you've ever thought about lying about your own age, just remember, age is only a number and these days everyone's got yours!

Paul Newman Made Me Do It

It was my first time. Yes, I know it's unusual for a 60-something year old woman, but I'd never really felt the urge before, never felt compelled to do it, never succumbed to its allure, never knew the joy it could bring. But there I was, a middle-aged Jewish woman trimming her first Christmas tree.

Growing up in a predominantly Jewish neighborhood, buying, owning or trimming a Christmas tree was never an issue. Our streets just didn't appear on Santa's map. There were no reindeer hoofs clambering on our roofs, no ho-ho-hos down our chimney and no little chocolate chip cookies waiting for Jolly Old Saint Nick. Instead, there were menorahs aglow in the windows, crispy potato pancakes sizzling in the kitchens and presents wrapped in shiny blue paper. And no one in my crowd ever owned the hybrid of all hybrids, the Chanukah bush.

So just how did I come to be decking the halls, fa-la-la-ing and tinseling a tree? Paul

Newman made me do it! No, it wasn't his blue eyes that got to me, his sumptuous salad dressing or tempting tomato sauce. It was Boggy Creek Camp and he was one of the founders. Camp Boggy Creek, located in Central Florida, is a haven for children seven to sixteen suffering from chronic and life threatening diseases. The camp offers summer sessions, weekend retreats and holiday parties for the children to "forget they have what they have".

"Camp Boggy Creek is looking for volunteers to decorate their recreation hall for a big Christmas bash this weekend," my friend Irene informed me. "Want to go?"

"Why not?" I responded.

A few days later, after a 45-minute drive through horse and cattle country, we arrived at the complex. It was a sprawling development with cabins, a horse barn, a sports and recreation center, a theater, a pool, and trained staff to normalize the children's lives, if only for a short while.

We were ushered into the huge rec hall just waiting to be turned into a holiday wonderland. A dozen bare trees stood around the room.

"Pick a tree, any tree," the director Robin said. "And there's plenty of decorations to use over there," she added, motioning to a huge pile of lights, Christmas balls, tinsel, angels, and garlands. "Let me know if you need any help."

I looked at the trees and decorations and thought, just how hard can this be? Millions of people do this every year. But just to be on the safe side, I said, "I'll take the one way in the corner," figuring my inexperience at yuletide decorating would be less noticeable there.

I walked over to the heap of decorations and dug into a big box filled with lights. It was a jumble of wires and bulbs with no seeming end or beginning. After wrestling with the wires, I was able to get an intact string studded with small white bulbs. It looked fine, but I had seen enough sitcoms to know you don't string any Christmas lights without plugging them in first. Into the socket they went and to my surprise, they all lit up! I was ecstatic. I unplugged the lights and painstakingly wove them over and under the limbs of the tree until I reached the very top.

Tinsel and Christmas balls were next. Round and round the tree I went in a decorating frenzy. By the time I put the angel on top, I was humming Deck the Halls and really enjoying the Christmas spirit. I began to imagine Santa putting presents under my tree and the happy faces of the Boggy Creek kids as they opened them. I could almost hear the clatter of hoofs and I was even tempted to leave a plate of cookies and milk for Old Saint Nick.

I stood farther back to admire my tree. I thought it was gorgeous, especially since it was my first one. I was *"kvelling"*—that's an old Yiddish word meaning beaming with pride and commonly used by parents in conjunction with their children's achievements, but it somehow fit the occasion.

As I marveled at my accomplishment, another volunteer tapped me on the shoulder.

"Nice tree," she said.

"Thanks," I replied happy that my handiwork had been noticed.

Then she got closer and whispered in my ear. "The only problem is, in order for it to light up, the plug needs to be at the bottom of the tree, not the top!"

Quickly and quietly, I went over to the tree hoping nobody would notice. I removed the string of lights carefully so I wouldn't disturb the delicate balls I had hung with such care. I rewound the lights around the tree making sure the plug was on the bottom. I straightened out the angel, threw on some more tinsel and finally plugged in the lights.

How beautiful it looked now with all the

lights a-twinkle. It gave me a warm and happy feeling and I knew that somehow, somewhere, both Santa and Paul Newman were *kvelling*.

ET, Phone Home Plate

I had never paid much attention to them before, but when their number suddenly began to multiply in my neighborhood, I began to worry about them. My next-door neighbor had had one for years, but I always thought he was a little far out anyway. But in the course of a few short months, almost every home—large or small, split-level or high-ranch—began to sport the small, gray, saucer-like dish on its roof. Are my neighbors trying to contact UFOs? Have ETs already invaded my neighborhood and trying to phone home? Has the population of Roswell, New Mexico moved to Yorktown Heights, New York and no one told me?

My curiosity was satisfied when my husband asked one day, "Lois, are you going to be home one afternoon this week so the satellite people can install our dish?"

Oh no, I thought, not him too!

"Are we trying to make contact with little blue men?" I asked.

"No," he said, "But I am trying to make contact with men in blue and white pinstriped uniforms who play at Yankee Stadium."

"What?"

"Haven't you heard? Don't you read the papers? We can no longer get the Yankees on cable TV," he said incredulously.

I *do* read the papers, but to tell the truth, I rarely read the sports section—arts and leisure, yes! Local news, yes! Book reviews, yes! Obituaries, yes! But not the sports section.

"What happened?" I asked, feigning interest.

"There's a dispute between the Yankees' network and Cablevision. The only way we're going to see the Yankees this season is if we get satellite TV. It won't cost much more but you will have to be home for them to install it. Is next Tuesday afternoon all right?"

"I never realized you were such a Yankees' fan," I said.

"It's really for Lawrence," he replied.

Lawrence! He'd said the magic word. Lawrence is our son who "temporarily" moved back home after an unsuccessful experience living with a roommate. It wasn't something we had expected, but after all, it was only temporary.

There was certainly nothing I wouldn't do

for Lawrence, even deal with saucers and satellites. Frankly, I'm a TV purist, a throwback from the old Dumont days. I'm a television dinosaur who is loyal to the local stations that gave us *Howdy Doody*, *Our Show of Shows*, and *Gunsmoke*. Only rarely do I jump ship and dally with CNN or HBO. As far as I'm concerned, just bring back those old rabbit ears. The oldies but goodies are good enough for me, but if it was going to make our son happy, I was willing.

"Okay, Tuesday's fine," I said not fully realizing what I was getting into.

And so, on Tuesday, I waited for the installer to beam the Yankees' channel and over 100 others to our house. Since I was only going to watch about one or two of them, I was less than excited.

The installer arrived in the afternoon ready to make contact with the netherworlds of TV.

"Three TVs to be connected?" he asked as he looked down at his work sheet. "One in the master bedroom, one in the second bedroom and one in the family room, is that correct?"

"I guess so," I answered as I watched him unload three black boxes to connect us to not one, but seven channels of HBO, five of Showtime, Cinemax, Starz, Oxygen and other worlds I had never explored before. He spliced wires, stretched cable, connected boxes, pressed buttons and in a few hours we were ready for take-off.

"Okay," he said, "Let's dial the office to get you operative."

"You have three boxes, is that right ma'am?" the young woman on the phone asked.

"Yes, that's right," I responded.

"What package did you want?" she asked.

"I don't know. What package did we order?" I said.

"I don't have that information," she responded.

Neither did I. I looked at the installer with questioning eyes. "What package do I want?" I asked him feeling very ignorant and out of the loop.

"Plus," he said, "Get plus."

"Plus," I said into the phone with confidence.

"That'll be $39.99 a month," she said, "Uh, did you want to get the local channels too?" she asked casually.

"What?" I said, "I'm getting 122 stations but that doesn't include the local channels? Those are the only ones I watch."

"That'll be an extra $4.99 per month per TV," she said. "Shall I include that in your plan?"

"Yes, yes, please," I said, immediately

thinking of what my life would be like without *CSI*, *West Wing* and *Everyone Loves Raymond*. Everything now set, I couldn't wait until the male members of my family came home to use the satellite.

"Mom," said Lawrence, "this is going to be great. We're going to have an on-screen program guide including previews and descriptions, a favorite channel list so we can find the shows we want fast, a menu and a mailbox that will send important information directly to the screen. And, we're going to have the Yankees," he shouted with glee.

He raced up the stairs and to turn on the set in his room. And I couldn't wait to see the smile on his face when his illustrious team was at bat.

"Mom," he yelled desperately, fiddling with the remote, "we're not getting the Yankees."

After all that, we're not getting the Yankees. How could that be?

"I checked the cables and they seem fine, Mom, and the boxes look properly installed. What package did you get?" Lawrence asked me.

"Plus, I got Plus. Isn't that what I was supped to get?" I asked.

He immediately picked up the phone and spoke to a satellite TV customer service representative.

"Okay, I see," I heard him say. "Yes, $59.99 each month plus $4.99 per set per month for local stations, fine."

So, now for $74.96 a month plus tax, satellite TV and the Yankees finally came to our house that evening. As I sat down to enjoy *CSI*, I was now the one who fiddled with the remote to no avail. I clicked and clicked only to receive one of those important messages directly on my screen. It read, "Scanning. The satellite is unable to get a clear signal."

There were a couple of signals I now wanted to give the satellite company.

"Lawrence," I yelled, "I'm not getting channel four!"

"You must have done something wrong," he said.

You got that right, I thought.

"Did you set the mode to TV and hit the power button, set the mode to satellite and hit the power button again?"

"Uh, huh," I replied.

"I don't know," he said, "I'm getting channel four on my set. Dad," he yelled to my husband who had just come in and settled himself in front of the downstairs TV set. "Are you getting channel four down there in the family room?"

"Yes," Michael replied. "Is there a problem?"

"Mom isn't getting it on her set," he said.

Michael came up to inspect the situation and just before he commandeered the remote, he whispered to our son just loud enough for me to hear, "Your mother just doesn't have a masculine side."

Then, he stood in front of the set and repeated the very same motions I had just made.

"See," he said brandishing the remote. "Set mode to TV and make sure it's always channel three. Hit the power button, set mode to satellite, hit power button and *voilá!*"

And after all his manly machinations, I got what I waited for all day—snow and static. No *ER*, no *Friends*, no *West Wing*, no Ray Barone being ridiculed by his mother, no Barbara Walters interviewing George Clooney ... just snow!

"So," I said, "I guess I'm the only one on the house who isn't getting the local stations?"

"Uh, looks that way," Michael said sheepishly. "It must be a loose connection."

Yes, I thought, the one in my head when I agreed to this out of this world satellite arrangement. Quickly, my dynamic duo checked all the connections and replaced the offending wire. Suddenly the familiar faces of Frasier and Niles Crane beamed up at me from the screen and I was at peace.

In the next room, the Yankees were in hot pursuit of the Twins. Lawrence sat very comfortably in front of the set and beamed as Bernie Williams batted one out of the park. He nearly jumped out of his seat when Jeter jolted one to left field. He was wide-eyed when David Wells wowed them at the mound. Sitting there with his remote, his satellite TV and his beloved Yankees, he was content.

And I got a clear signal that neither my son nor ET would be leaving our house anytime soon.

Spam I Am

I never wanted to try Spam™. Even though there are hundreds of recipes—including one for Spam™ cupcakes. Spicy chopped ham squished into a little 12 oz. can just never appealed to me. Actually, anything made of animal entrails doesn't appeal to me. Thank goodness it was one of the few things my mother never forced me to eat. Being Jewish and eschewing pork products, Spam™ was never brought into our house.

But even being Jewish doesn't prevent Spam from being a part of my life now. Every day Spam enters my house whether I want it or not. No, not the kind that comes in a tin, but the unwanted, unsolicited email messages named after the ubiquitous luncheon meat.

These messages can be just as mysterious to me as actual Spam, and just as spicy. Just this morning, 'BernieMaddoff2' wanted to help me earn 36% annually on my financial holdings. 'Victoria38DD' wanted to send me a cream to increase the size of my other assets and

'RandyRandy' wanted to enlarge a piece of anatomy that I don't even have.

Yesterday my email box was filled with 14 messages. One was from my son detailing his vacation itinerary; one from my nephew giving me directions to his new home; and one was a political cartoon from a friend. All the others were Spam invading my time and space. One was an offer for "free" cellular service; another for a "free" vacation; and 'PonceDeLeon1512' wanted to help me reverse the aging process and look ten to twelve years younger.

Not only does Spam have the power to pop up of its own free will, but it has the power of spontaneous reproduction as well. No matter how many messages I click into my trash can, they are replaced by double the amount the next morning. Maybe they should be called "rabbits" instead of Spam for their ability to multiply so quickly. Maybe they should be called "kittens" because they turn up in multiples in a basket and nobody wants that many, if any, in their house.

"Jeff," I said, speaking to my son on the phone, "all this Spam is driving me crazy. Isn't there something I can do?"

"Mom," he said, "you can put a trash filter on your email message list. It will filter out words and phrases that are generally safe to send to Spam heaven. Anything that contains dollar signs, exclamation points, or a series of "xs" would fall into that category. Into the garbage can will go messages that contain the words *university diplomas*, *Viagra®*, *free*, *win*, *ground floor*, *fat burn*, *stop smoking*, *make money*—and of course anything from your friends 'RandyRandy' or 'Victoria38DD'."

I installed the filter and now I don't have to waste my time clicking Spam into the trash. I have time to download a map of Ireland to see where my son will be vacationing; purchase a housewarming gift for my nephew; and exchange some political humor with my friend. I may even have time to check out that recipe for Spam™ cupcakes!

A Full Nest

They are the words every empty nester dreads to hear: "Mom, I've decide to move back home." But these were the very words I heard from our own twenty-four-year-old son, Lawrence, a few years after he graduated from college.

Trying to remain calm, collected and supportive, I replied, "Great, you know we love having you home." And that wasn't a lie. We enjoyed having our adult son home for one, two, maybe three days … tops.

"It's just temporary," he said. "To give me time to save some money, regroup and find a new roommate."

Temporary … how I hated that word. It was just temporary when we moved into our first home, a small fixer upper. We temporarily lived there for seventeen years. Just how many years was our son going to temporarily stay with us?

"I really can't stand my roommate," he said.

"You mean the roommate with the

incontinent dog? The roommate who punches holes in the walls every time the Mets lose a game? That roommate?" I asked, not able to control the "I told you so" tone of my voice.

"Yes," he said, "he's such a slob."

Since I considered Lawrence our very own Oscar Madison, I didn't even want to think about the slovenliness of his roomie.

"Really?" I said as I remembered the half-eaten, petrified sandwiches in his closet and the mound of dirty socks under his bed when he left for college.

"Yes, Mom. He leaves dirty dishes all over the place and his room is a mess."

Now where had I heard those words before?

"I've started packing up my stuff and should be home in a few weeks," he said.

"Great," I replied. Great—it had been five years since he had left home to go to college and a year since he moved in with his roommate. A lot of things had changed since then.

We had turned his bedroom into our TV room, complete with comfortable easy chair and hand-made afghan. We had shampooed the carpet and repainted the walls. We'd replaced his heavy metal band posters with peaceful Monet prints and his picture of Michael Jordan with a photograph of the last summer's cruise to

Alaska.

Despite our trepidation, a few weeks later our son moved back in lock, stock and amplifier. Actually, it was amplifiers—three to be exact, one of which weighed more than I did. Our family room, used for watching old movies and quietly sitting by the fireplace, was suddenly transformed into a music room, complete with not one but two guitars, the three amps and a keyboard. His extensive collection of CDs and videotapes lined the walls of his reclaimed room. The easy chair was pushed into a corner and became a silent butler for his clothes. The afghan disappeared.

After such a long absence, it was strange to have this man-child back in the fold. When he had lived far away from home, my worries about him were generalized. I didn't know where he was all the time, who he was with, what he ate and drank, and that was probably a good thing. Now that he was home, the worries became more specific.

"Cold pizza for breakfast, Lawrence?" I asked. "Wouldn't you be better off with cereal and juice?" "Is that jacket warm enough for today?" And I simply couldn't bring myself to fall asleep until I heard his key in the door, even if it was at three o'clock in the morning.

We quickly found out that we needed a set of ground rules so as not to invade each other's space and privacy, and to preserve each other's dignity. Lawrence would be responsible for his laundry, cleaning his room and for putting his dirty dishes in the sink (putting them directly into the dishwasher was way too much to ask). He was to tell us if he wasn't coming home for dinner or if he was going to be away for any length of time.

My part was to try not to treat him like a child, which is hard for any mother to do regardless of the age of her son or daughter. I reluctantly resisted the urge to put bleach in his graying laundry and to remind him to take his lunch to work. I didn't ask him if he was dating anyone new or urge him to take an umbrella on a cloudy day. This was just killing me! It went against all my maternal instincts.

It didn't take long to realize that a lot had changed in five years, especially our son. Lawrence was always on time for work and well respected at his job. He was a helpful friend and a thoughtful, insightful human being, coming to the aid of his friends and family. It was hard to believe that this responsible, caring, mature adult had been the same child I'd had to roll out of bed each morning for school, the child who didn't hand in his assignments on time.

His clothes were now classy and well maintained. Could this be the same child who had worn nothing but black t-shirts and steel-toed boots to high school for four years?

He discussed politics and scientific breakthroughs at the dinner table. He taught us about his work doing market research. Could this be the same child who barely mumbled hello to us all through high school?

Somewhere between New York and Atlanta, our fledgling had turned into a mature man. I knew that sometime soon he would pack up his amplifiers, CDs, and videos again and head out on his own. I started to envision moving the easy chair back in front of the TV set in his room. I imagined being bundled up in the afghan and watching *ER* and *60 Minutes*. But before I got too carried away, there was an important phone call I had to make. I dialed our older son's number.

"Hi, Jeff," I said. "How are you?"

"Fine, Mom," he replied.

"I just called to ask you a question."

"This sounds important," he responded.

"Oh, it is," I said. "How's your roommate?"

Discussion Guide
Book Clubs and Discussion Groups

1. In *Trying on Bathing Suits*, the author rues the day the *Sports Illustrated Swimsuit Issue* comes out. How much influence does the media have on your self-image and self-worth?

2. *Final Resting Place* explores end-of-life options. If you were given the option of being frozen and then thawed out when a cure for your demise was available, would you want to do it? Why or why not?

3. The Information Highway has made it possible to find out almost anything about anyone – without their permission. In *It's Just a Number*, a friend's age is revealed even though she wanted it kept secret. How do you feel about what the author did? Have you ever been tempted to do the same?

4. In *Paul Newman Made Me Do It*, trimming her first Christmas tree fills the author with pride and a sense of accomplishment. Do you have something to *kvell* about?

5. In *Leaf Me Alone*, the author is confused by her neighbor's lack of action. Have you ever had a problem with a neighbor and how did you handle it?

6. *Trying on Bathing Suits & Other Horror Stories* reflects on problems that happen to all of us. Did anything in the book make you say, "Yes, that happened to me"?

Born and raised in Brooklyn, Lois Podoshen spent most of her adult life living in Yorktown Heights, New York. A freelance writer, she recently relocated to Central Florida. She is the author of four children's books published by Richard C. Owen Publishers, Inc.: *The Birthday Bird*, *The Artist*, *Paco's Garden* and *Grandpa's Candy Store*.

Her feature articles have been published in *Westchester Magazine*, *Westchester Weddings*, *Westchester Family* and *The Westchester Jewish Chronicle*. She also writes advertising copy for *Hudson Valley Magazine*.

In her former lives she was a New York City elementary school teacher, a marketing manager for a publishing company and tutored foreign students.

Lois hates trying on bathing suits but loves to laugh, especially at herself.

Made in the USA
Lexington, KY
10 July 2013